CONNECT
···· WITH YOUR ····
INNER
SPIRIT

CONNECT
— WITH YOUR —
INNER
SPIRIT

Rise to The life of Your Dreams

MARIA SIBILLA

CONNECT WITH YOUR INNER SPIRIT
RISE TO THE LIFE OF YOUR DREAMS

iUniverse books may be ordered through booksellers or by contacting:

iUniverse
1663 Liberty Drive
Bloomington, IN 47403
www.iuniverse.com
1-800-Authors (1-800-288-4677)

Because of the dynamic nature of the Internet, any web addresses or links contained in this book may have changed since publication and may no longer be valid. The views expressed in this work are solely those of the author and do not necessarily reflect the views of the publisher, and the publisher hereby disclaims any responsibility for them.

Any people depicted in stock imagery provided by Getty Images are models, and such images are being used for illustrative purposes only. Certain stock imagery © Getty Images.

ISBN: 978-1-5320-8251-1 (sc)
ISBN: 978-1-5320-8252-8 (e)

Print information available on the last page.

iUniverse rev. date: 09/27/2019

For My Source/Higher Power and my Family.
Thanks for all the support.

INTRODUCTION

Do you ever feel like there's more to life than what you're currently living? Do you ever wonder what your true purpose is, what you're really here on this earth for? Are you lacking peace or direction? Are you struggling or needing change in any area of your life?

I felt all of these things and asked all of these questions, and I got the answers I was looking for. There's a lot more available to you than you know. We're all spiritual beings living a human experience, meant to be plugged in and connected to our higher power/God/the universe/our true selves. Learning to connect opens us up to divine guidance and direction. When we take the time for spiritual health, it will lead to good health in every other area of our lives.

My hope is to help you like so many great teachers and mentors have inspired me through various books and courses that I've taken. With these easy-to-read chapters, I give you techniques, skills, and processes that I've used and continue to utilize today. These skills have helped me tremendously in my life, and you can easily do the same to create lasting change, leading you to the life of your dreams.

I'll teach you what I have done, what I continue to do in my own life, and what I have taught many others for years.

These tips have helped me to change and transform my entire life in a positive way.

In my experience, you have to go deeper spiritually before you can rise up higher in your thinking and living. We're all part of the higher power/God/the universe, and that great spirit lives within each and every one of us. You have to tune in to find what you need, want, and desire. You have a great power available to you.

I hope these words bless you and help you on your journey through life.

Namaste (my soul salutes your soul)!

CHAPTER 1

CONNECT

Learning and knowing how to connect with Source/God/the universe/your inner true self is by far in my experience the single-most important thing that you can learn to do in your life. Available to everyone, it's a skill that can be learned and transcends all barriers despite age, race, religion, or gender. It's love in its purest form. Some learn this young; others realize it old. A few never learn it, which is a shame.

I learned this at a young age. I've felt spiritually in tune since childhood. I've always felt like I had access to a different world, so to speak, like an invisible grace and goodness that I could actually communicate easily with. Not everyone could see it, but I could.

This is a place I could easily access often. I learned later in life through reading and researching that I was born in tune, that is, sensitive spiritually. I used to enjoy being alone and playing by myself as a child because I wasn't really alone. My family always said I was a dreamer who liked living in my own world. Because I was dreaming and creating, I was writing, thinking, and communicating with Source. I grew up in a prayerful home. My parents believed in God and prayed, so that was also an example I saw.

Having this skill to connect with divinity would prove to serve me well in my life, although it would not shelter me from life's normal turbulence. I'm glad it didn't, because the turmoil made me who I am today. I now know they were lessons that taught and shaped me into who I am now. The skill to connect would serve as a constant calm in my life, one that is invaluable to me and the greatest thing I can teach you for your life.

Learning how to come to this calm refuge is lifesaving sometimes. When life gets hard for you—notice I said *when* because life is full of ups and downs, hills and valleys, for all of us at one time or another—that's how we learn, grow, and expand. And that's what we came here to do.

You don't have to be afraid of life's experiences, but it does help if you are armed with a little arsenal of tips, skills, and techniques to make your existence go a little smoother. My hope is to help you on your journey through your life. It doesn't matter where you are in your experience. There's never a wrong time to learn to connect to Source/God/the universe/your inner true self.

CHAPTER 2

FIND YOUR PEACE, CALM, AND CENTER

Learn to find your peace, calm, and center within. Try to start here every day, and come back to it often. All answers, everything you could imagine, are here in this place. If you don't have your peace, calm, and center and don't know how to get grounded, then you have nothing. You must learn to get and try to stay grounded, or you can lose everything and anything that you've worked for or that has been given to you. For me, this is without a doubt the most important step in the process. Start here, and keep coming here often to keep your peace. We can aim to try to stay in this place of peace, calm, and center, but life happens.

When you really learn to experience this, it's almost a dreamlike state, as if you're actually somehow removed for a bit from this human world that we live in because you are connecting with your spirit. Your body is receiving calming and healing benefits from it, but your spirit is leading the experience. Once you learn the skill of tapping into this—and everyone and anyone can learn this—you will be able to get calm quickly and easily with practice.

This is available to everyone, and once you learn how to meditate, pray, and connect, you'll find that it's like learning any new skill. You'll get better in time. Be patient with yourself while learning this. Prayer and meditation are the ways to a healthy spiritual life. In fact, studies show that they benefit us physically, mentally, and emotionally as well.

Taking the time to connect can only help you. Nourishing your spirit is something you do through prayer and meditation. Just as you feed your body with healthy food, water, vitamins, and exercise and your mind with knowledge, you should also take the time to nourish your spirit.

You're a spiritual being meant to be plugged in and connected with your energy source, to experience all that is meant for you. There's an abundance of everything available to you, whether it be peace, direction, a higher level of thinking and living, love, or anything you could ever imagine. It makes me wonder, *Why isn't this taught, or why is it a mystery to so many?*

I know what you're thinking. *There are so many people who look so happy and successful without thinking about their spirits, praying, or meditating.* That may be true for some people, or maybe it just appears to be that way. You aren't that person. You were made to be connected or close to spirit. You were made for something more! That's why you feel the pull and why you're so curious and searching. You know in your heart and spirit that there's a higher level of living waiting for you.

This is a process, and you can't expect everything to happen immediately. Over time, like a seed that's planted, tended to, and nourished, it will grow, and you will reap a harvest and see amazing results in your life. You will not be disappointed.

Meditation

Meditation is quite simple, and anyone can learn to do it. It's recognizing how to clear your mind of all thoughts, especially the wrong ones, so you can relax, be calm, and really be in the present moment, allowing you to be open to receive guidance, wisdom, or anything else that you might need.

Meditating is healthier for your mind, body, and spirit then living in a state of mind that is always frantic and worried. I know this from experience because I used to live my life like that. It didn't feel good. I was always trying to do it all and forgetting myself. But I changed and transformed my life little by little into a much healthier, peaceful, balanced one.

I prayed consistently and learned to meditate and practice yoga, which includes a lot of breath work. I wrote in my journal every day, read self-improvement books, studied, and applied what I learned. I utilized positive quotes and affirmations and listened to my inner spirit. I put the work in, and step by step, I was guided, directed, and led. I showed up consistently every day with an open mind and heart, trusting, believing, and having faith in my higher power, and it worked. I've learned and have grown so much, and I want to share it with you.

When you can put yourself in a relaxed state, you'll find that you have genius, creativity, guidance, answers, wisdom, and an abundance of everything inside of you already. You have to learn to be still and quiet the mind to access it. Meditation is a simple skill that anyone can learn, and the more you practice it, the easier it is to get to that calm space, even in the midst of chaos going on around you. I've read a lot of books on meditation and studied and practiced it for years, and I am so much healthier and happier in every way because of it. There's scientific evidence that it changes your body chemistry and is life changing.

Meditation is simply sitting calmly and blocking out everything around you for a period of time so you can experience an inner peace and be in the present moment. It doesn't have to take long. Here's how to do it:

1. Sit in a quiet room with no distractions.
2. Close your eyes. Block the world out. You can put on soft, calming music if you want to. I like to sit in silence.
3. Repeat the same mantra over and over just to keep focus. It doesn't matter what it is. The point is that you are focusing on one word or phrase to keep other thoughts out, clearing your mind, calming yourself, and keeping yourself in the present moment.
4. Take deep breaths in through the nose, hold for ten seconds, and then push out through the mouth, concentrating on your breathing. Do this five times. This works wonders when you're anxious.
5. If you feel your thoughts drifting away, gently bring them back to the breath. Feel your mind being emptied.

You can also do guided relaxing meditations. You can watch them on YouTube, listen to CDs, or take meditation classes.

Make time for meditation daily or several times a day. I promise you that the more you take the time to practice meditation and be in the present moment, it will become easier for you to do. The benefits are amazing and can be life changing.

It's best if you have the time to sit until you feel the peace inside of you. Try to get to this peaceful place before you do anything else. Always come back to this place as needed for rejuvenation. This is where your true power is.

Prayer

Talk to God as if you're having a conversation with a friend. Ask questions and write them down. Listen for answers. Sometimes responses come right away; other times they take time. But when they do, write them down. They don't always make sense at the time until you look back later, and then they make perfect sense. The more that you pray or meditate, the easier it will get. Prayer becomes a communication. It's a relationship, a give-and-take. It's truly something you can rely on. God/the universe/spirit never leaves you. The only time you feel distant is when you push it away and don't realize you are not tuned in, but you can always get the closeness back any time you want to. Just ask.

You don't have to be afraid. There is nothing to fear. God is a loving God, nonjudgmental, healing, and accessible. He doesn't push anything on you. It's more like gentle guidance and suggestions. You're worth it, and this is for you. I know life is confusing sometimes, but it helps to have someone on your side. You have always felt in tune spiritually, sensing things most others can't, things you can't seem to explain. You have a sensitive spirit, and you feel a pull like there's something more for you to do, a quality greater than yourself. You know this in your heart because it's true.

You're meant to be plugged in and connected, and this will open you up to divine guidance, direction, peace, calm, love, healing, support, and an abundance of everything. This power is listening and available, and it wants to help you. We are all called for a purpose, and our job is to find out what that purpose is.

The healing grace is extraordinary and starts in your spirit. Then it seeps into all other areas of your life. You won't be disappointed, but you have to go deeper spiritually before you can rise up higher in your thinking and living. Just start with tiny steps and have faith in the process.

Remember that the practice of prayer and meditation is simple and anyone can learn to do it. The more you practice it, the easier it becomes, making it easier for you to get to a calm space, even in the midst of chaos going on around you. It's about learning how to clear your mind of all thoughts, especially negativity (wrong thoughts). I call these thoughts random surface thoughts that aren't from the divine. Once relaxed, you can really be in the present moment, allowing you to be open to receiving guidance, wisdom, peace, love, or anything else that you need from your higher power/your true self.

Prayer and meditation are good for your spirit, mind, and body. It's an amazing feeling to be able to put yourself in a relaxed state, allowing you to experience what already exists within you. You have to learn to be still and quiet the mind. If you're not relaxed, you'll clench up and block the flow. The flow is where you want to be.

I've studied and practiced this for years, and I'm so much happier and healthier in every way because of it. I literally made this my way of life and part of my daily routine years ago, and it was one of the best things that I ever did. Make the decision to make this a habit. Subtle changes happen in the beginning, and then over time you will experience amazing, beautiful changes in yourself and your life.

CHAPTER 3

TUNE IN AND LISTEN TO GOD/HIGHER POWER/ INNER WISDOM

Be gently and divinely guided. God tries to get our attention in so many different ways:

- a song playing with just the right lyrics
- other people saying the perfect thing you need to hear at the right moment
- a thought in your own mind
- a persistent notion that keeps coming up and doesn't stop
- your intuition, feelings, or a hunch

Calm down, listen, and be patient. This takes time. If you want guidance on your true purpose, destiny, journey, or with any area of your life, you will get it. There is no doubt. Just listen.

When you connect with your higher power/spirit/the universe, you're putting yourself in a position to receive. You show up, and you are willing and open. What do you receive?

+ ideas that you didn't even know you had
+ new visions for your life
+ gentle guidance
+ direction for all you were meant for
+ the position of your true purpose where you're given the talents, skills, and abilities to perform these tasks

Don't believe me? How do you think I'm writing this book? This is all divinely guided action from the notion that I actually have an idea, want to write about it, and think it's worth reading, pushing through fear, and taking the massive steps needed to go through this book-writing journey. Trust me. This is not my power alone.

Oftentimes God tries to lead you, but you're not tuned in or paying attention, so you just shrug it off. You don't understand the clues. Sometimes it's that you're afraid or you don't feel like there could be something better for you. Thankfully God is very patient and waits for us to get it.

When I was being guided to write this book, I would hear the same messages over and over in my head until I wrote them down. Then I would get more, and they would swirl around in my head until I wrote them down. I asked God, "What am I supposed to do? What is my true purpose?"

We all have a lot of things that are important to do, whether it be being a mother, wife, friend, daughter, sister, dog owner, or whatever the case may be. I was at a time in my life when I was asking, "What is my bigger purpose?" I felt like there was something else that I was supposed to do. It was a divinely appointed job because we all have one. I was told that I would write books to help girls. To be completely honest with you, that wasn't really what I wanted to hear, although that is a very noble thing.

I thought, *Really? Why do I have to do it?* But I have a strong faith and reverence for God, so I listened. I was told that I wouldn't be disappointed, that I would be greatly rewarded, divinely guided, and supported through the entire process. And I have been.

There is a great power behind you when you take divinely appointed action. The only way you can discover yours is by going within, listening, and trusting. If you don't have the faith, pray for faith. Just say, "Please let me have faith and trust in you, God. Let me be willing to try." One by one, divinely guided connections appear at just the right time.

Appreciate

Start with appreciation for where you are now and all the things that you currently have in your life. Stop and think of a few things every morning. Write them down and feel thankful for what you're thinking of. You'll end up writing more than a few things, and doing this will shift your mindset to a positive one, raise your vibration, change your energy, and clear out negativity.

As you practice these steps, it will become easier for you to do. It will become so easy that peace, calm, and centered feelings will be the natural state for you most of the time. You will feel so much better. Appreciation will give you immediate relief from any stress you are having in your life. Make it your intention to start here every day upon awakening and end with appreciation every night. It opens you up for more and is another way to connect.

Journal Writing

Begin writing in a journal every day, preferably in the morning or when you find the time. Don't worry about grammar or spelling. This is just for you to read. It's for your eyes only. One of the purposes of journal writing is to get your thoughts out of your head so you can think more clearly. It also organizes and sorts out your thoughts so you can think of what you want in your life.

God can communicate to us through prayer and meditation but also through our writing. Write your questions and prayers down, and you will get answers. You might not understand what you're writing at the time, but jot it down anyway. It will make sense to you later.

I try to write at least six pages every day of free writing, where I just put pen to paper without stopping or editing. It's something that most writers do. I learned about it in a writing class years ago. It's surprising how after you get all the random thoughts out of your head, you then tap into your true self/higher power/creativity/inner genius, which we all have inside of us. Creativity and your best thinking begins to flow.

By taking the time to consistently pray and meditate every day and connect to your higher power/God/the universe, you will become spiritually in tune, which will lead to better health, happiness, and abundance in every area of your life. If you would like to experience some changes in your life, even if it's simple modifications, or if you want to become the best version of yourself, then take the time to connect within your higher power through prayer and meditation for guidance on anything you could possibly need or want. Take the time to go deeper spiritually so you can rise to a higher level of thinking and living.

Everything you need is already inside of you. You have divine guidance, love, and support all around you, waiting and wanting to help, but you have to ask God/the universe for help because you ultimately have free will, and nothing can be pushed upon you.

If you do ask, you'll get gentle nudges, answers, guidance, and inspiration like I did. For me, it's writing, so I would write the same thing. Then, I started a blog and put everything into posts. I put my blog into the world for others to see and read. Then, I just got more inspired ideas and things to write about and act on. Have faith, and you will constantly and continuously be led in the right direction for your best life. Don't worry about fear. It's completely normal, and everyone experiences it. Push through it. The other side feels glorious. You deserve this. It's for you.

CHAPTER 4

GET YOUR THINKING RIGHT

If you change your thoughts, you change your life. You probably have heard this before many times. It's not a new concept, but it's one that really provides success, if you work it. Change your words and actions. Get rid of stinking thinking.

Thoughts are so powerful that they literally create things and your reality. You have to clear out all the random thoughts that pop into your head all day long. I call these thoughts "surface thoughts." They don't really matter, and a thousand times a day, they pop into your head and change your feelings, emotions, mood, and reality. The good news is that you can deliberately change your thoughts. You get to choose what you think! Isn't that amazing? Why doesn't anyone tell you that early on in your life? You have to wait until you self-sabotage for years. Then, you hear about books like *The Secret* by Rhonda Byrnes, *Awaken the Giant Within* by Anthony Robbins, or countless other self-help books that tell you, "You are creating your reality with your thoughts that you're thinking." Wow! It's true.

Positive thoughts change your vibration and energy. They lift your spirits. Choose thoughts that deliberately make you feel better, and once you do, you'll attract what you want. You create your own reality. I know it works because I consistently live my life like this. While it's not always easy, it's another skill to learn. Tried and true, it absolutely works. I think some people do this naturally without even thinking about it, and a few of us have to learn it.

When learning to change your thinking, you have to give yourself permission to draw a sacred circle around yourself while you heal because you'll go back and forth a lot at first. This is a totally new concept for you. You're retraining your mind to think new thoughts. Keep the world out. You can be your own worst enemy, and so can the world's views and attitudes toward you. It's important that you become elevated in your thinking by learning the truth about yourself and who you really are.

Clear your mind of negativity by replacing it with positivity. This isn't easy, and it takes time, but you can do it. You can be so hard on yourself sometimes. The world around you can be so negative. Just turn on the news. You're instantly bombarded by all the bad things that happen in the world, rarely the good. You have to consciously reprogram your thinking to change your life. It's not to be callous or uncaring. It's to protect your energy from being drawn into despair. You have to keep reaching for a better feeling thought to keep your vibration, energy, and yourself up. Especially if you're a sensitive person, you can actually take on other people's energy. You will do no good to yourself or anyone by shrinking down, but you can be the light in the darkness for yourself and others by rising up. You have to recondition your thinking and speaking in order to see change in your life.

Thoughts and words are so powerful that they can be a breeding ground for sickness and disease or greatness and triumph. Your thoughts lead to words, and what your ultimately thinking will show up in your life like seeds being planted. When you purge your mind of a negative thought, you have to immediately exchange it with a positive one. It's impossible to be thinking a positive and negative thought at the same time.

Positive thoughts and affirmations are a great way to set the intention for the day. When you go to bed at night, read a few of your favorite quotes. While you sleep, these good thoughts will be planted into your subconscious mind. When you wake up the next morning, do the same thing. Set a positive affirmation by reading some quotes and being grateful for a few things.

Remember if you don't like your life, change your thoughts—one thought and one word at a time. Consciously be aware of what you're saying to yourself all day every day. Find good in every situation, no matter how bad the circumstances seem at the time. Look for reasons to feel good and be thankful and happy. Tell yourself a new story and create a new life.

CHAPTER 5

CHANGE YOUR VIBRATION/ENERGY

Your personal vibration/energy is the vibe that you give out to the world, the vibe that resonates with you. I've read numerous books on this topic, and what they say is true: the thoughts—a single one, in fact—that you think literally changes what you feel and transforms your personal energy/ vibration. If you can control your own thoughts, you can create your own world and attract good things to yourself.

The vibration and energy that we are giving off at any given time is attracting everything to us in our lives without us realizing it. Controlling your thoughts sounds easy to do, but it's not always easy because we live in a world with other people, circumstances, and situations that interfere, so to speak, with our thoughts, which then affect our feelings. Then you know the rest. It's vibrational interference. Our thoughts and feelings then start to attract things that we do not want into our experience. Ugh!

So to control your own thoughts is to have great power and control over your life. How do we control our thoughts consistently? How do we become masters of this? There is a way. There are great teachers and leaders, alive today and throughout history, who have mastered this great skill.

They say that our thoughts are just things, and if we step back from them, we realize that the thoughts are not who we are. We are love and light and also part of God. Our thoughts are just things that come and go. Observe them. They will just pass. Let them go, and choose another good thought and feeling.

Learn to put yourself first. Make yourself the most important person in your life. Unfortunately, we're not taught this as young women. As women, we're taught to be caretakers and nurturers, thinking of others before ourselves. We are taught to be nice, kind, and sweet. This is great, but not everyone in the world plays by the same rules. Not everyone wants to be nice, kind, and sweet nor care about your best interest. Some care about their best interests first. So it's necessary to put yourself first as a woman.

Some girls learn this early on. They have no problems expressing themselves and communicating their hopes, dreams, and feelings to others. They have loud voices and strident energy, and they have boundaries in place where you wouldn't dare cross. Some of us have to learn this skill the hard way, but it can be attained.

It's your job to control your life and your energy/vibration. It's your responsibility, not anyone else's. It's your job to look at your dreams and goals, to make your own choices and decisions, and to think your own thoughts. Don't be willing to change for someone else. Once we find our strength within, our confidence, and our self-esteem, we can then lead by our calm and confident manner, which is more powerful in the end. Sometimes you find it and lose it, but you can always get it back again by going to the calm place within yourself. Work on yourself first!

Write Lists

Another way I tend to my vibration and keep up my energy is to write lists. Writing lists makes you feel organized and in control, and it's empowering to cross off items on those lists. Thinking about future goals and writing them down gives you something to look forward to. Doing these things will get you in touch with who you really are and what you want. These skills will help you sort out your thoughts so you can then set up healthy boundaries because you know what you do and don't want. You can find your voice to speak out, tell others no, and be comfortable with it. Say, "That's not what I want!" You can do it in a way that you're comfortable with because you're sure of yourself.

When you know who you are and what you want and communicate it clearly to others, they are less likely to try to control you, manipulate you, and push you around. This is your life, and you get to decide how you want to live it. Period. I know this is hard sometimes depending on where you are in your life. It was for me. It's especially difficult when it's natural for you to be nice. But being nice doesn't mean that people can push you around. When you continually go inward to find strength and courage, draw from it, and apply it to your own life, things will start to change. Find the strength and courage for you.

These are some of the things that I find to be helpful to myself:

+ Spend time in nature. It's very grounding. Be outside with the earth below your feet. Being around trees, sun, and wildlife is healing.
+ Walk, exercise, stretch, practice yoga, breathe, drink lots of water, and eat clean. Do any kind of exercise. Just keep moving.
+ Help others without forgetting yourself. It always makes us feel better when we open our hearts to help someone in need. Give without expecting anything in return.

The practice of self-care will help you to get in touch with who you really are and what you want, which is incredibly empowering, and it will raise your vibration.

Life is truly a journey, one that can be wonderful. It's supposed to be for us. But we have to take the time to learn these skills. All of this has been life changing for me, and I hope it helps you too.

Remember, it's your responsibility and your job to tend to your vibration to experience all you want in your life and to live the best version of you. It's pretty simple to do if you know the tips, skills, and techniques that I've shown you. Always put yourself first so you can be your best and be the best for others in your life. Practice self-care and keep your vibration/energy raised. You won't be disappointed.

CHAPTER 6

HEAL FROM YOUR STRUGGLES (EVERYONE HAS THEM)

The only way to heal from your struggles is to forgive yourself and others and move on. Get out of the trenches. Stop circling around in the wilderness now. It was a lesson, not a death sentence. I'm sure you've heard all this before, but sometimes we need to hear it again because we forget.

We all have struggles at one time or another, in one way or another. It's inevitable. In this life you live, this journey you're on, you will not escape without them. So the important thing to remember is to try to stay calm, work through a struggle, and not stay stuck for too long. That's the tricky part sometimes.

How do you get unstuck? Remember that it's only temporary. Life has ups and downs, hills and valleys. Only you can gauge and monitor your progress because you are the only one who knows the best way to live your life. If you don't, ask a trusted friend, teacher, mentor, or counselor, someone you look up to and preferably a person who knows you well.

Try to separate yourself a bit from the problem. Try to rise above it as if you're looking down on it. In this time of your life, ask, "What steps can I take to move past this?" Write down your thoughts, questions, and answers. Pray about it. Ask to see it through God's eyes. Pray for help with it. Some say, "Cast your cares on God to feel relief." It actually says that in the Bible.

Whatever it is, you will survive, rebuild, grow, and expand. You will fight and be strong. You're tough and courageous. Be brave. You will endure and dream again.

Life throws us curveballs when we least expect them and then another, as if trying to teach us something. In fact, that's exactly what it is doing. Knowing this makes it a little easier once you get through the struggle and recover. Enduring these struggles can sometimes be almost unbearable depending on what you're going through. Everyone has struggles that are unique to them.

No one can know the time it takes to go through a particular situation, but trying to strengthen yourself and build yourself up before and after is key. Be strong in life, and try to put yourself in good situations; always be able to expand, grow, and learn. Have a well of strength, a place where you can draw up what you need.

It's like filling your tanks. If the tanks are full, you have reserve to draw from. If the tanks are empty when you need to draw up from them, you'll feel depleted. Even worse, it will leave you feeling like you're going to crack. Try to prepare yourself to soften life's blows by setting up some cushions. If your tanks are full, life's blows don't seem as hard as they do if you're already depleted. So fill your tanks.

There are warning signs when you start to get low. Get to know yourself and listen. It's different for everyone. No matter where your stress and anxiety levels are, the approach is the same. If you're feeling a little off-balanced or in a deep depression, you feel like you're drowning. Life is best if it's balanced. Whatever that means to you, everyone's version of a balanced life may look different. You have to learn about yourself. Whether you're thriving or just surviving, you need to nurture yourself. Consistently take baby steps every day.

Most experts say that these are the four areas that must be nurtured to keep balance: spiritual, mental/emotional, physical, and financial. Deep within yourself is a reservoir of strength, might, fight, power, courage, wisdom, and anything else you could possibly need, want, or desire, but you have to learn to access it.

You are not this situation that you're in. You are much more than that. Despite what anyone else says or thinks about you, you know deep within your heart and soul who you really are. Your inner true self knows. Visualize that person right now, the best version of you, the individual you can see with your mind's eye. See it and feel it. Hold on to that.

Forgive yourself and others so you can move on and be free. Give yourself that gift. Let the past go. Look at the past as a series of events that taught you some lessons. Separate yourself from the events of the past and the future. Don't worry about the future, and live in the present—right now. It's incredibly freeing when you can do this. It takes off the pressure. This doesn't mean you should be neglectful and not plan. While you're working, moving, and planning, don't obsess over the past or the future, but rather be present in the moment. Enjoy the occasion.

Forgiving others doesn't excuse their bad behavior, and it doesn't mean that the person has to be in your life anymore. You can set up the boundary that you see fit for you. Forgiving is trying to understand the person from his or her level of understanding. Not everyone is at the same level of growth and expansion, and again, this doesn't excuse bad behavior. It does help you to know that that person has a different level of understanding. He or she has had a totally different past experience than you did. Looking at it this way helps you to have compassion for other people, and then you can let the experience and sometimes the person go. You can be free.

Forgive yourself for past mistakes, because you were only working with what you knew at the time. Let it go. Be healed.

CHAPTER 7

LEARN TO DREAM

Imagine and visualize. What do you really want to show up in your life? Visualize often and be a dreamer. You should always have a dream, a goal, or a vision of something that you're moving toward. When you have your mind-set right, ideas will flow. A dream will keep you motivated and your attitude positive. It's healthy to dream. If you don't, you'll become stagnant and depressed.

Dream big. You're allowed. It's a dream. Go as big as you can and then go higher. You don't have to tell anyone about your dream. As a matter of fact, don't. It's for you. Remember daydreaming as a child? It wasn't small. Why does it have to be microscopic now? Why does it have to be what some people call realistic? It doesn't. You're a creative person with big ideas. Dream, imagine, and visualize.

Your dream might seem so far away from where you are right now. It may never seem attainable, but it's good for your mind to dream. If you keep it in your mind and set goals, even if they're little ones, continue moving in the direction of your dream every day. It will become reality. Eventually it will come to pass. I know because it's happened to me many times.

Write down your dreams, goals, and visions. If you've read other things that I've written, then you know how important I think it is to jot everything down, whether it's a daily journal, your thoughts, lists, or goals. I'm constantly writing lists. Something happens when you take your thoughts and write them on paper. It makes them more concrete, they're good to look at, and it keeps them fresh in your mind.

Setting Goals

The size of the goal doesn't matter. You just need to focus on something that fuels you. Ask yourself:

1. What can I do every day to move toward my goal?
2. What can I do every week to move toward my goal?
3. What can I do monthly to move toward my goal?
4. What can I do quarterly?
5. What can I do this year, next year, three years from now, four years from now, five years from, and so on?

Where would you like to see yourself? Remember to do this every day so you don't forget about it, preferably in the morning and evening. Thinking, dreaming, and getting your mind-set right is more important than taking the physical steps to your goals. Mind-set is everything.

Be encouraged and proud of yourself every step of the way. Don't look at your limitations. Just look at your dream and who you are in the dream. Everything starts in your mind. Winning and losing is in your mind. All battles must be won in your mind first before victory will ever show up in your life. You have to see it and achieve it in your mind first. Make this a priority.

You know deep within who you are and what you're meant for—that's why you get frustrated sometimes. You yearn for what you know is rightfully yours. You may have just forgotten. It just hasn't shown up yet, but it will. Be patient. It's coming.

Who are you? What are you meant for? Why are you here?

You're spiritually in tune to be close to God/the universe/Source and understand the things of God. It's a gift. You're a vessel for the blessing. You're a co-creator with a great team behind you, and you don't have to rely on your own limitations because this doesn't come from you. It comes through you. You're here to live your best version of yourself, live in abundance, and help others.

You can create the life that you want to live. Create little goals, habits, and routines that you do every day that add up to big results. Creating these habits puts you in a position for success.

It doesn't matter how big or small they are or what they are. Your goals are yours. The important thing is that you have them, even if it's just one.

Be specific. What does the goal look like to you? Establish a plan and ask yourself how you can get to your goal. I like to break things down into little pieces. What do you need to do? Give yourself realistic deadlines. Begin with the end in mind and go backward. Give yourself credit for coming up with a goal and a plan! Yes, you can do this.

Visualization

I love visualizing. It's such a powerful tool. There's scientific proof that it actually changes your body chemistry. You can feel a shift in your energy when you visualize, focus on an image that you're enjoying, or visualize and imagine a dream, something you want to happen in your life. You're not denying what the current situation of your life is. You can love the life that you're currently living but aspire for more. Aspire to learn, grow, and change and also have great experiences in your life.

Visualize every detail of what you want to experience. Actually feel yourself living in this situation. Visualizing puts you in a state of allowing. Experts say that your subconscious mind can't tell the difference between reality and an imagined vision. When practiced, it will eventually become your reality.

Believe that you can achieve your goal. This might take some time depending on where you are on your life journey. You have to think positive, and if you don't, then start retraining your mind to do so because this will stand in your way if you don't. If you dream and visualize your best life but think negative thoughts, you will cancel out all the work you've done.

Don't underestimate what you can accomplish. When done consistently over time, momentum begins, and you will be moving closer to your life goals. I personally use this approach all the time in my life.

Be your best supporter and encourager. Be happy with your results as you move forward into the direction of your dreams. Always appreciate where you currently are while looking at where you're going. Also look at where you are now and where you've been. As you make progress, no matter how small, be proud of yourself for the results your producing. Feel the progression. Be grateful.

Find a Mentor

A mentor should be someone you can look up to. Observe to see what they are doing, not to envy or copy, and surround yourself with people you aspire to be like. They say that you become the sum of the five people you are with the most. If you don't physically have people in your life that you would like to be like, then find these mentors in books or podcasts. Follow people on social media who inspire you to be better. Stop procrastinating and making excuses rather than decisions.

Take creative action with daily steps toward your life's goals with consistent habits and routines that add up to big results and successes over time. You'll be happy that you started.

You deserve it. You can do it. Believe in yourself. You're stronger than you think you are. Don't beat yourself up if you have a bad day. It's completely normal. Just readjust and start again.

CHAPTER 8

GET OUT OF YOUR WAY

Believe, Receive, Accept, and Say Thanks

Feel like you already have what you desire. Allow it to come to you. Stop pushing it away. It's yours already. Whatever you are seeking is seeking you.

There is a higher level of living and thinking available to you if you want it. But it is a choice. You have to first believe and then actually receive and accept it. That can be hard sometimes.

Be thankful and humble, which ultimately brings more to you. Keep what God has given you and be faithful with it. Appreciate it. Say that again. Realize that your abundance comes to you from God/Source/the universe. It is your divine right.

Stay focused and connected. Once you learn how to connect, plug in, and tune in, you have to try to stay there. Just like exercising the body, staying connected is a spiritual exercise. You have to stay connected and continue to do your spiritual exercises to keep what you receive and to keep growing. You won't be perfect at this, and that's okay. You'll learn to get better at it.

This is a prayer that I say:

> While I'm feeling appreciation for being blessed right now, I'm thinking about the power and magnitude of God/the universe/ Source, and I am humbled. I am open to receive all the love, power, blessings, and abundance that God has for me. I feel the flow and thank God.

I ask, "What do you want me to write? What do you want me to do today? I am a team member with you, a co-creator. What is your will for me today?"

You have to let it flow to you and through you. Don't push it away. Feel it in your heart and spirit and every fiber of your being, and be thankful before it even shows up. It's one thing to believe in a higher power but another to connect. That's the first place to start. You have to also allow, receive, and accept the blessing by letting it flow to you—do not push it away. Sometimes we do this and don't even realize that we're doing it. You have to keep your mind-set on right thinking.

Sometimes you don't let yourself get blessed. You pinch yourself off. You ask, and then you're afraid. So you don't allow it. You keep asking for the same thing over and over, not understanding why you're not receiving your heart's desire. Either you don't feel that you deserve it or you don't believe in the higher power that wants to bless you.

You don't realize what you have. God/Source/the universe created you; therefore, your part of God, and God is love and a creator. God is brilliant and abundant. And so are you. This is hard to understand sometimes, but it's true. An abundant God wants to bless us. It's easier to start by asking for little things, and then your faith grows from there.

You deserve to experience the life of your dreams. It isn't going to happen all at once, but it will occur if you ask, believe, say thanks, and allow it. You will get everything that you want, all of your heart's desires. You are loved, guided, and protected.

Think of something that you want. Start with something small. Follow these steps:

1. Ask God/the universe/higher power for whatever you want.
2. Believe. This is hard sometimes because you have to believe in the abundant universe/God that wants to supply everything for you.
3. Ask for faith and help in believing.
4. Receive and accept it in your head, heart, and spirit. Feel as if it's with you already.
5. Say thanks, be grateful, and appreciate that it's been given to you already. It's done.

Now wait for it to show up, but while you are waiting, don't ask again, because it already has been given to you. Don't keep focusing on the absence of it. This can be a little hard sometimes. Trust the process. Have faith that it's on its way. You can be excited about the anticipation, but don't keep asking. It's on its way. It's yours already. You deserve it.

All your heart's desires are coming to you when you allow yourself to be blessed.

The Secret of Manifesting Your Desires

Before you can manifest what you desire, you have to feel it. They say to visualize what you want. You have to believe it and be thankful for it, but honestly, there's really more to it than that. You have to feel it. Everything that anyone has ever achieved and received in life was once a thought and a vision. In fact, the world began with a thought. You have to spend time imagining your desire so much that it's real before it happens.

It starts in your mind as a thought. It starts with mind-set.

CHAPTER 9

YOU'RE AN INSTRUMENT

You're part of a bigger plan. You're a channel, a vessel, and a receiver. You have a true purpose, a life's purpose. Let God use you. The gifts you were given are from God. You were given these gifts to enjoy but also to give away to others. They come through you. They're not for you to keep. You have a job to do, and you'll be given everything you need for your divine job. When you think of it this way, it takes a lot of the fear and worry away.

Everything leading up to this point has been preparing you for your purpose. This is hard to comprehend sometimes. We have insecurities and self-doubt. You have to continually keep your thinking right in order to accept, receive, and not block the flow.

Sometimes you just have to take a leap of faith and trust. You have to get out of your comfort zone, trust the process, work hard, and have patience to be prepared, positioned, and provided for. Give it away. More will come. When you are in line with your God-given true purpose, you will be supplied. The same ideas will keep coming until you act on them, and then you will receive more. There's no shortage. When you're connecting, there is abundance.

Blessings come to you to enjoy but also to give away. Think of yourself as being a piece of a puzzle. You don't have to concern yourself with anyone else's puzzle, just your own. You're an instrument in the orchestra. You just have to play your part; you don't have to worry about anyone else's. I find it incredibly freeing to think of it like this. I'm not in charge of this big plan. God is. I'm just doing my little ole part. That's it—just doing my part and getting blessed abundantly.

Don't lose hope. There's always hope, even if you can't see it. Never give up. You can create the life that you want to create, the life you dream about, even if it seems so far away. Remember that you're a creative person that wants to create.

1. Begin with the end in mind. Search your soul for what you want. What sort of life do you see your ideal self living? Write it down, and look at it often. See it. Feel it. You'll have it.

2. Be happy and joyful, and have fun along the way at whatever stage you're at. Don't resent where you are. Don't despise small beginnings. Appreciate and be thankful for all of life's lessons. Life is a process and a journey, and in some ways, you're better than you were before. Even though you're not exactly where you want to be, appreciate something about where you are now while enthusiastically looking forward to where you're going.

3. Have the courage to get what you want. Don't be afraid, and even if you are, do it anyway. Push through the fear and get to the other side. Be strong.

CHAPTER 10

TAKE ACTION

Nothing is going to happen in your life if you don't take action, and if you're following the ideas in this book, then you'll need to take inspired action. You have two choices in life: accept your life the way it is or change it. It's your decision. Taking action is the scary part. It's the part that makes you feel so uncomfortable. It feels really good when you're soul-searching, praying, meditating, and digging deep within spiritually, and these are all very important growth experiences.

There comes a time when you need to put yourself out there and take massive action. Sometimes we think it's going to be worse than it really is, but then it's not as bad as we thought. Whatever it is that you need to do, you just have to jump so you can experience more growth. You have to. It's the next stage in your progression. Otherwise, you stay where you are forever, never realizing your true potential. You know that's not what you want, so go for it.

Success leaves clues. Learn to look for them. You were meant to shine your beautiful light for all the world to see.

In conclusion, remember the following:

1. The first thing is to connect with your true spirit within your true self, who knows you deeply. Do this daily. You are part of God/Source/the universe.
2. Next, always find your peace, calm, and center. Know how to get and stay grounded.
3. Make sure to tune in and listen to divinely guided inspiration that is being transmitted to you.
4. Get and keep your thinking right. Maintain positive thoughts only.
5. Keep your vibrations/energy high. Know how to raise them.
6. Heal from your struggles. Move past them and be free.
7. Dream, visualize, and imagine your best version of yourself living the life of your dreams.
8. Get out of your way. Stop blocking the flow.
9. You're an instrument, vessel, conduit, receiver of the blessing, and part of a bigger plan. It's not just about you.
10. Take action to move to the next level of your growth.

I hope that you found some inspiration and something meaningful to you in my words. My hope is that this book will bless you and help you on your journey through life. Always remember to be strong and courageous. If you follow the techniques that I've given you, take the steps, and learn the skills, they will become a habit, and a new way of life will happen for you. Your life will only get better. It can be transformed, changed, and definitely made a little better. "I wish you all the best".

Maria Sibilla

Printed in the United States
By Bookmasters